KEEPING THE BEST
A practical guide to retaining key employees

D1555826

Other titles from IES:

Getting the Best out of your Competencies
Strebler M T, Robinson D, Heron P
IES Report 334, 1997. ISBN 1-85184-260-8

Skills, Competencies and Gender: Issues for Pay and Training
Strebler M, Thompson M, Heron P
IES Report 333, 1997. ISBN 1-85184-262-4

Changing Roles for Senior Managers
Kettley P, Strebler M T
IES Report 327, 1997. ISBN 1-85184-255-1

Personal Feedback: Cases in Point
Kettley P
IES Report 326, 1997. ISBN 1-85184-254-3

Outsourcing: a Flexible Option for the Future?
Reilly P, Tamkin P
IES Report 320, 1997. ISBN 1-85184-247-0

A catalogue of these and over 100 other titles is available from IES.

the | **Institute**
for | **Employment**
| **Studies**

Keeping the Best

A practical guide to retaining key employees

Stephen Bevan
Linda Barber
Dilys Robinson

Supported by the
IES Co-operative Research Programme

Report 337

Published by:

THE INSTITUTE FOR EMPLOYMENT STUDIES
Mantell Building
University of Sussex
Brighton BN1 9RF
UK

Tel.   + 44 (0) 1273 686751
Fax   + 44 (0) 1273 690430

British Cataloguing-in-Publication Data

A catalogue record for this publication is available from the British Library

ISBN 1-85184-265-9

Printed in Great Britain by Microgen UK Ltd

The Institute for Employment Studies

IES is an independent, international and apolitical centre of research and consultancy in human resource issues. It works closely with employers in the manufacturing, service and public sectors, government departments, agencies, professional and employee bodies, and foundations. Since it was established over 25 years ago the Institute has been a focus of knowledge and practical experience in employment and training policy, the operation of labour markets and human resource planning and development. IES is a not-for-profit organisation which has a multidisciplinary staff of over 50. IES expertise is available to all organisations through research, consultancy and publications.

IES aims to help bring about sustainable improvements in employment policy and human resource management. IES achieves this by increasing the understanding and improving the practice of key decision makers in policy bodies and employing organisations.

The IES Co-operative Research Programme

This report is the product of a study supported by the IES Co-operative Research Programme, through which a group of IES Subscribers finance, and often participate in, applied research on employment issues. The members of the CRP are:

BAA plc
Barclays Bank plc
British Broadcasting Corporation
British Steel plc
BT plc
Cabinet Office (OPS)
Department of Health
Department of Transport
Electricity Association
Glaxo Wellcome plc
Guardian Insurance
Halifax plc

HM Customs & Excise
Inland Revenue
Lloyds TSB Group
Marks & Spencer plc
National Westminster Bank plc
Post Office
Rolls-Royce plc
J Sainsbury plc
Shell UK Ltd
Unilever UK (Holdings) Ltd
Woolwich Building Society

Contents

1 Introduction

1.1 Downsizing and retention: strange bedfellows?

Many organisations in the 1990s have concentrated their efforts on reducing costs by reducing their headcount. For some, this has meant very dramatic programmes to lose staff, and to change the basis of the employment relationship they have with those that remain. Amid all the activity to 'right-size' organisations, however, has been a bubbling concern over unwanted losses of key people in key posts.

In fact, in many companies there is a growing concern that the loss of even a small number of key employees could have serious business consequences. This is especially the case in functions or business units where commercially sensitive work is conducted, or which employ staff with a high market value. It is for these key staff groups that traditional approaches to staff retention are widely felt to be inappropriate or ineffective. In addition, for their line managers, the risk of losing key people in key posts creates a strong sense of vulnerability.

1.2 Demands on HR

Within HR departments this creates a number of problems:

- HR professionals have a duty to be responsive to line management concerns, though in some of these cases, there is often little evidence that there is an existing retention problem.

- Line managers frequently articulate their analysis of the problem (and therefore the solution) in terms of pay. HR professionals know that these problems are rarely as simple as this, but line managers want quick solutions rather than more analysis.

- HR professionals also know, however, that if they ignore warnings of imminent losses, they will get the blame when key staff actually leave. In addition, line managers will begin to question whether they actually have as much local autonomy as the business has led them to believe.

- However, if HR professionals did respond to every call for market supplements and other special payments, they run the risk of corrupting parts of the pay system, paying out when it is not necessary and, at the same time, opening the floodgates for other managers to 'bid up' the value of their key staff in an attempt to redress internal inequalities.

It is likely that a proportion of the concern that exists over this issue is underpinned by an unrealistic view about the average service an organisation can realistically expect to get from specialist staff, as well as a sense of effrontery when somebody **does** choose to leave.

1.3 Increasing labour market buoyancy?

In addition to these growing concerns *within* organisations, the labour market is showing signs of recovering some of its former buoyancy. We are not talking here about a return to the haemorrhaging of staff, experienced (together with skill shortages) by employers in the mid to late 1980s. Nonetheless, conditions now appear more favourable for those employees with high market value who, for whatever reason, wish to change employer.

- According to UK employers' own estimates, as many as one third of vacancies are proving hard to fill, and the trend is rising. The proportion of employers affected by recruitment difficulties rose to almost one-third in 1995. The impact of hard to fill posts has again roughly doubled in only 24 months.

- The number of registered, unfilled vacancies in the UK currently stands at their highest level since November 1989 (Labour Market Trends, 1997).

These shifts, together with a perceived erosion of job security, may prompt individuals who feel they have market worth to try their hand at a new challenge.

The Institute for Employment Studies

1.4 Keeping the best

This document is a short guide for employers. It provides some ideas and help for those who are experiencing retention problems among key employees, or who anticipate doing so. It examines:

- why retaining key employees is likely to become a major business issue in coming years
- how employers can tell if they have a problem, or are at risk
- why key employees choose to leave
- what can be done to keep them longer.

There are no magic answers to the problem of staff retention, but this document seeks to demonstrate that employers *can* have an impact by putting into place a number of simple preventative measures and approaches.

2 Why Worry About Retention?

In recent years, the recession has had the effect of depressing the labour market. High unemployment, coupled with the apparent failure of the 'demographic timebomb' to explode, meant that every advertised vacancy resulted in a flood of applicants. The recession followed a boom period during which unemployment was low, and the labour market worked to the advantage of job hunters. The experience of the past decade has reinforced the belief, held in many organisations, that it is the economic climate and the labour market that causes staff turnover rates to rise and fall; the employer is at the mercy of external influences, unable to change the situation for the better. The intention of this chapter is to show that:

1. the labour market is regaining some its former buoyancy, allowing increases in staff turnover rates

2. that such increases can have serious consequences for employers of highly marketable employees.

We begin by looking at the external factors which provide the context within which the mobility of labour is increasing.

2.1 External influences

Here we will look at the following factors:

- demographic change
- the changing labour market
- latent turnover
- changing people, changing work patterns.

2.1.1 Demographic factors

The UK's demographic structure is starting to present challenges to employers, not only with regard to younger employees, but also towards the older end of the workforce. Figure 2.1 illustrates the projected changes between 1993 and 2006, in the age profile of the population of working age.

There are already reduced numbers of 16 to 24 year olds entering the workforce, which means that employers who have traditionally targeted recruitment at school leavers or graduates may have to re-think their approach. This much-heralded demographic 'timebomb' failed to make much impact during the years of recession, but there are now signs that it is, if not exploding, at least fizzling. For example, projections for Great Britain for the year 2006, compared with 1992, show that there is likely to be a decrease of 1.4 million people aged under 35 in the labour force.

The same set of projections also show a predicted increase, by year 2006, of 2.3 million people aged 35 to 54, and 0.7 million aged over 55. The post war 'baby boomers' are now in their late forties, and will soon be entering the last decade of their working lives. Many of them, having seen what happened to their older

Figure 2.1 Age profile of UK labour force, 1993-2006

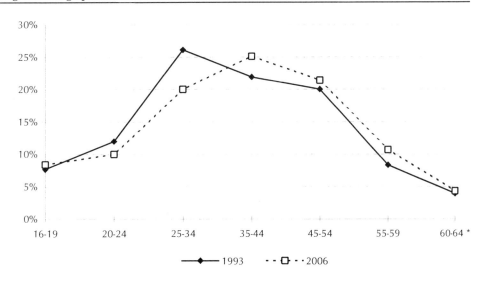

Source: Employment Gazette, April 1994

colleagues during the recession, may have an expectation that early retirement choices will also be available to them. While this may be a useful option to employers who are downsizing, others will find that their organisations cannot function without their '50 pluses'. A recent article in the *Health Service Journal*[1], for example, featured Portsmouth Healthcare NHS Trust, which has a large bulge of staff in the 45 to 50 age bracket, and comparatively few employees aged 25 and under. The Trust has recognised the potential problems which such a large early retirement bulge could create, and is targeting retention initiatives at this age group.

2.1.2 The labour market

Although recovery from recession has been slow, there are definite pointers that the labour market is picking up. Unemployment has fallen fairly steadily over the past two years; the average claimant unemployment rate in the UK during 1993 was 10.3 per cent, compared with the current (mid to late 1996) rate of below eight per cent. Another pointer is that the number of registered unfilled vacancies in the UK currently stands at their highest level since November 1989 (Labour Market Trends, 1997).

More employers are also starting to report recruitment difficulties. At first, these tended to be specific and caused concern mainly because they were occurring in key specialist areas. More recent evidence points to a more general increase in turnover rates. The *Skill Needs in Britain* surveys report a steady annual increase from a low point of ten per cent in 1992, to 11 per cent in 1993 and 11.5 per cent in 1994. The 1995 figure jumped dramatically to 21 per cent, although the 1996 figure of 14 per cent would seem to indicate that 1995 threw up a statistical blip; discounting 1995, the general trend still seems to be on the up. The 1996 survey indicates that turnover is highest in:

- the London area (19 per cent), followed by the South East (16 per cent) and Yorkshire and Humberside (also 16 per cent)
- the distribution and consumer services sector (23 per cent)

---

[1] *Health Service Journal*, 6 June 1996, 'Workforce Planning: Keeping the baby boomers on board'

The Institute for Employment Studies

- organisations with between 25 and 49 employees (17 per cent) — although the largest organisations (500 plus) have experienced the biggest rise in turnover between 1994 and 1996 (8.9 to 12 per cent).

There is an argument that employees no longer stay loyal to one employer, so traditional retention initiatives are doomed to failure. While it is true that job tenure has fallen, the trend is not dramatic. Median job tenure has fallen since 1975, particularly among men (see Figure 2.2), though it has increased among women. Many people do, in fact, stay with their employer for prolonged periods. In 1993, for example, over half of those in full time work had been with the same employer for more than five years, and around one third for more than ten years (Labour Force Survey).

2.1.3 Latent turnover

With a more buoyant labour market, employers also need to face up to the possible threat posed by latent turnover. During the recession, many employees may have wished to leave their organisation and move elsewhere, but the economic climate has prevented them from doing so. There is a danger that pressure is building up in some organisations, and that a big improve-

Figure 2.2 Estimated median job tenure in months (present job), 1975 to 1995

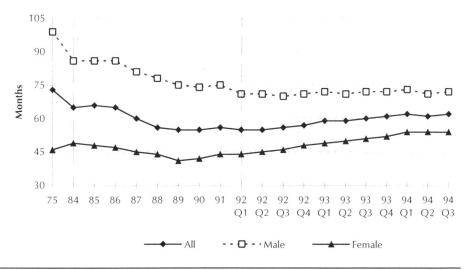

Source: from Employment Policy Institutes, Employment Audit, Issue Two, Autumn 1996 page 18-19 tables 2 to 2b

ment in the job market may lead to a sudden exodus of staff as they realise their ambitions at last. This may have some healthy consequences — unhappy and frustrated employees can sometimes be destructive to the organisation — but the loss of a large number of employees, or a small number of key employees, over a short space of time could cause far worse problems.

Understanding Intentions

IES has considerable experience in running employee attitude surveys, on behalf of organisations both in the private and public sectors. These surveys usually ask about employees' career intentions, as intention to stay or leave the organisation is one indicator of employee satisfaction or dissatisfaction. The information gained can help employers gauge the extent of latent turnover in their organisation.

For example, an attitude survey of employees in a large retail organisation, conducted in 1995, revealed that ten per cent of staff planned to leave within six months. Although this percentage is not unduly high, it helped the organisation to know that leaving intentions were not evenly distributed around the organisation. Only five per cent of area managers, for example, planned to leave within the next six months, compared with 11 per cent of shop assistants and an even higher 14 per cent of head office staff. A similar question in a survey for a large department of a leading investment bank (1996), revealed a discrepancy between managers and staff; no managers, but 16 per cent of staff, planned to leave within the following six months.

2.1.4 Changing people, changing work patterns

There is considerable evidence that today's employees are facing a different set of domestic responsibilities from those of their predecessors.

- The number of people aged 80 and over in the UK more than doubled between 1964 and 1994, to 2.3 million (*Social Trends*, 1996).

- In a recent study, one in six employees had eldercare responsibilities (Help the Aged, 1995).

- By early 1994, one in six working people was a woman with a child under 16 (Sly, 1994).

- The proportion of employed mothers in 'professional or managerial' jobs nearly doubled during the 1980s (Harrop and Moss, 1994).

- Almost three-quarters (73 per cent) of a predicted rise of 1.5 million in the labour force by spring 2006 are women (*Labour Market Trends*, 5/96).

- Twenty per cent of children live with only one parent (*Social Trends*, 1996).

The above trends have contributed to a change in the desired patterns of working, away from the traditional full-time job towards more flexible options. These changes must be recognised if problem levels of labour turnover are to be tackled. An increasing number of organisations are adopting 'family-friendly' or 'carer-friendly' practices, in an effort to keep their employees. The following flexible options are all on the increase.

- **Part-time working:** part-time workers represented 24 per cent of the working population in 1995, compared with 14 per cent in 1971 (IER).

- **Flexible hours:** 11 per cent of employees in the UK in 1995 came under some form of flexitime arrangement (Atkinson *et al.*, 1996).

- **Teleworking:** this enables employees to work from home, often at times which suit them best.

Another way of recognising domestic responsibilities is to offer appropriate terms and conditions — school time contracts, for example, or eldercare leave, or childcare vouchers.

2.2 Consequences of turnover

For most organisations, turnover can have a number of serious consequences. Of course, the consequences of staff turnover can be serious even if the volume of leavers is low. Although most of the consequences are negative, we should not be fooled into thinking that staff turnover is always a bad thing. Indeed, zero turnover can be as much of a problem as turnover in double figures.

Figure 2.3, illustrates the main positive and negative consequences.

On the positive side, staff turnover:

- allows the organisation to undertake a degree of re-structuring, as vacant posts provide the opportunity to make changes to the shape of sections or departments

Figure 2.3 Consequences of turnover

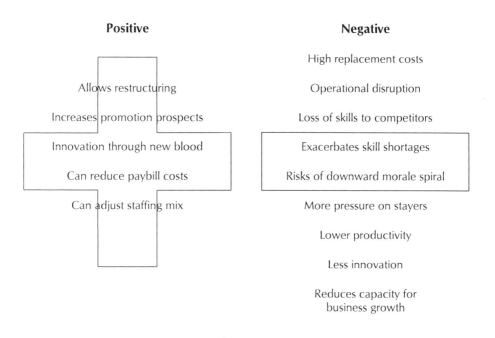

Positive	Negative
	High replacement costs
Allows restructuring	Operational disruption
Increases promotion prospects	Loss of skills to competitors
Innovation through new blood	Exacerbates skill shortages
Can reduce paybill costs	Risks of downward morale spiral
Can adjust staffing mix	More pressure on stayers
	Lower productivity
	Less innovation
	Reduces capacity for business growth

Source: IES

- can increase the promotion prospects of internal applicants, by creating vacancies in key posts

- can, alternatively, allow the organisation to fill a post, which might normally have been filled internally, with 'new blood' from outside the organisation. This may promote new ways of working

- can reduce paybill costs. As replacement staff can often be less experienced than the leaver, their initial employment cost can be lower. For example, many schools with delegated budgets have deliberately replaced experienced leavers with more junior (and, therefore, less expensive) staff

- can help organisations adjust their staffing mix. A full-time post can be replaced by part-time posts, job-sharers *etc.*, providing greater flexibility of resourcing.

On the negative side, turnover can have the following consequences:

- It can mean incurring significant replacement costs, especially if the post is difficult to fill, or if new starters need a large amount of training, or if the 'opportunity costs' of having a less experienced replacement is high.

- It can cause significant operational disruption, particularly is a leaver has been involved in, or running, several projects or tasks.

- It can result in the loss of key skills, knowledge and experience to competitors. In some sectors, considerable resources may have been invested in developing products, technologies or processes. Losing people who can ensure that the organisation gets a healthy return on this investment can be very expensive and commercially difficult.

- If the organisation is having difficulty recruiting key skills, the effects of losing employees who already have these skills can be doubly troublesome.

- If a core reason for turnover is employee dissatisfaction, turnover can have serious 'knock-on' consequences for morale, especially among those who might like to leave but, for a variety of reasons, are unable to.

- If staffing levels have been reduced, and if workload has increased, a number of leavers can increase the pressure on those who remain. This might, in turn, increase their own propensity to leave.

- In addition, the productivity and creativity of a workforce which can see turnover increasing, can also diminish.

- In some manufacturing or service contract businesses, staff turnover levels can be high enough to impede their ability to take on new work.

It is still common to find organisations who tolerate what, elsewhere, might be considered unacceptable levels of turnover, merely because they are unaware of its consequences. Under-standing these consequences is often one of the first steps in realising the benefits of keeping it under control.

3 Is There Really a Problem?

This chapter aims to equip the HR practitioner with a variety of diagnostic tools which can be used to assess whether or not the organisation has a turnover problem — and, if it has, where the problem is located. The areas covered are:

- measuring labour turnover
- making comparisons
- analysing the risks
- attaching costs to turnover measures.

3.1 Measuring labour turnover

3.1.1 Organisational beliefs

Most organisations have a stock of received wisdom about labour turnover. The following statements — which tend to shift the responsibility for turnover away from the employer — will probably sound familiar:

> 'We always lose a third of our trainees once they have qualified.'

> 'We're bound to have higher than average turnover — we employ lots of young women.'

> 'Turnover is higher here than at our other office/hospital/factory down the road, because of the antiquated working conditions here.'

> 'Our wastage rates are increasing because we can't keep pace with our competitors' reward packages.'

The power of these arguments is such that departing employees may even find themselves quoting them at exit interviews; it is, after all, easier to give comfortable answers that the interviewer expects, than to analyse and present the true reasons for leaving the organisation.

The HR practitioner can do little to explode turnover myths without making a start by calculating the true wastage rates within the organisation.

3.1.2 The overall wastage rate

The first step that is usually taken is the calculation of the organisation-wide wastage percentage — sometimes called the global rate. The formula is:

$$\frac{\text{No. of leavers in a given period}}{\text{Average staff in post over the same period}} \times 100$$

The period in question is almost always a year, although shorter or longer periods can be used if appropriate. To avoid anguish, the 'average staff in post' can be calculated by adding together the number of staff in post at the beginning and end of the period, and dividing by two.

Unfortunately, the overall wastage rate, despite being the one most frequently quoted, has two major disadvantages.

- It masks differences within the organisation. These may be biographical differences (gender, age, ethnicity) or employment differences (grade, function, department, job, length of service, location).
- It includes both voluntary wastage (resignation) and involuntary wastage (retirement, end of fixed term contract, dismissal, redundancy).

3.1.3 Specific wastage rates

The first thing to do is to remove involuntary wastage from the calculation. Involuntary wastage is obviously relevant for some purposes — *eg* in workforce planning exercises, such as calculating replacement rates — but it is largely out of the organisation's control. The voluntary resignation rate is the most relevant factor when considering the need for, and the nature of, retention strategies.

Secondly, in order to understand wastage properly, it has to be broken down into specific and more manageable chunks. The HR manager is advised to spend some time in exploring wastage around the organisation, to find out what factors are and are not relevant. Some factors have been shown by research to be particularly important in predicting high or low wastage. Age is one of these; wastage tends to decrease with age. Length of service (which is, of course, often strongly correlated with age) is also a well-known predictor; the longer people stay, the less likely they are to leave.

It is very likely that several factors will be found to be relevant to explaining differences in voluntary wastage rates around the organisation. Uncovering these will take some time, but will equip the HR manager with valuable information — not only for the satisfactory purpose of de-bunking some myths, but also as the basis for deciding whether retention initiatives are worthwhile, and where they should be aimed.

3.1.4 Some caveats

You will need to exercise some caution in interpreting your wastage rates.

- Low wastage is not necessarily a good thing. It might lead to promotion blockages, frustration and a lack of 'new blood' coming in to re-invigorate the organisation.

- A high wastage rate could be the result of a relatively small number of posts turning over repeatedly, rather than a pointer to a general problem. Calculating the **stability rate** can help to uncover this. The stability rate, like the wastage rate, can be calculated both organisation-wide and for specific groups. It can be calculated in different ways. One formula is:

$$\frac{\text{No. of staff at end of the period with } > \text{a given length of service}}{\text{Average staff in post over the period}} \times 100$$

As for the wastage calculation, the period taken is usually a year. The 'given length of service' could also be a year, but could vary depending on the organisation and/or the type of work involved. Normally, high wastage would be expected alongside low stability, but it is possible for both of the percentages to be high, indicating problems with a small number of high turnover jobs.

- Beware of small numbers, particularly when breaking specific wastage down into increasingly small groups. A wastage rate of 50 per cent may look high, but means very little if it is the result of one leaver from a department of two people!

3.2 Making external comparisons

Trying to work out whether your organisation's wastage profile is better or worse than that of your competitors is not an easy task. It is worth making the attempt however, as it could highlight areas where your organisation is doing particularly well or badly in wastage terms. This, in turn, could lead to an examination of the causes for the apparent anomalies, and to the uncovering of both, good practices that could be applied more widely, and problem areas that could respond to HR or other initiatives.

3.2.1 Benchmarking

Some published sources of labour turnover information are quoted in the *Employee Development Bulletin*, March 1996. The more useful of these are listed below.

- *APAC* (Audit of Personnel Activities and Costs) national HR database, published by MCG. This uses data obtained regularly from over 260 organisations from the private and public sector.

- IPD labour turnover survey results, published by IPD in the autumn of 1995. This contains data from 211 organisations which participated in a postal survey during March 1995.

- National management salary survey, published in April 1995 by Remuneration Economics, with the Institute of Management. This used data from 19,444 managers employed by 328 organisations.

- National management salary survey — smaller business review, published as above. This contains information gathered from 2,229 managers in 112 companies with a turnover of under £25 million.

- *Skill Needs in Britain*, latest version published in December 1995 by Public Attitude Surveys on behalf of the Department for Education and Employment. This uses data obtained via telephone interviews with 4,005 organisations, conducted during April to July 1995.

- The Local Government Management Board publishes data gathered from surveys of particular groups of staff — *eg* the annual LGMB teacher resignations and recruitment survey.

- Computer staff salary survey, published by Computer Economics in November 1995. This uses data gathered from a survey of IT specialists employed in 504 computer installations.

Although it can be very comforting to compare one's organisation to others, there are some caveats which need to be understood.

- The definitions used may not always be the same. A small difference in wording could lead to a big difference in the wastage rate quoted.

- The time period used in the data gathering exercise may not be appropriate for your organisation — calendar year versus financial year, for example.

- The way employees are grouped may not lend itself to comparisons with your organisation.

- External comparisons may lead to a false sense of security. If your organisation's wastage rate has increased markedly from the previous year, a problem is indicated — no matter how favourably it compares with your competitors' rates.

3.2.2 Networking

Fellow HR professionals in other organisations can be a rich source of information about comparative wastage rates, and could be a particularly useful source for comparative data in similar businesses, or in a particular geographical area. Bear in mind:

- The caveats contained in the section above.

- The need to respect confidentiality.

- The requirement to give information as well as to receive it.

3.2.3 Internal data sources

Your organisation's own information systems may help you with comparative information. An examination of data on source of recruitment and destination on leaving, for example, could allow tentative conclusions to be drawn, regarding whether your organisation is a net gainer or loser in terms of joiners and leavers. This information could be particularly valuable when considering key, highly valued employees.

3.3 Key people and key posts

Every organisation has its key posts and key people, each of which often warrants special attention when it comes to monitoring labour turnover and devising retention strategies.

Key posts can exist at all levels of the organisation. They can be defined as those posts which need to be occupied by competent people, and which cannot be kept vacant if the organisation's core business is not to suffer. At a senior level, the strategic importance of such posts is often recognised by the existence of a succession plan, to enable immediate substitution if the current post-holder leaves.

Key people can be defined as such for a variety of reasons. Often, they are experts in a particular field whose expertise may be of particular value to a competitor — but they could also be the organisation's visionaries, or skilled people managers and motivators. One group of key people is sometimes described as 'corporate glue' — those whose knowledge of the company's procedures, employees, history and core business make them invaluable advisors and reference points. Graduate trainees on accelerated promotion schemes are often categorised as key people, by virtue of the enormous amount of time, attention and money that has been invested in them.

Risk analysis can help to quantify the seriousness of losing key people, or of key posts becoming vacant. Appendix 1 details the use of a simple spreadsheet to calculate the retention risk of some key employee groups. The process to be followed is described below.

- **Step 1** — identify an occurrence which could present problems, *eg* your IT expert leaving to join your main competitor.
- **Step 2** — estimate the likelihood of this occurring. You could use a three point scale (low , medium or high risk) or, if you want to be more sophisticated, devise a scoring system which accounts for age, service and qualifications (*eg* factors commonly associated with leaving 'risk').
- **Step 3** — estimate how serious the effects would be of such an occurrence, using the same scale as in step two, on such factors

as the impact of a resignation in product/service delivery, the ease of replacement, replacement costs, and the advantage to competitors.

- **Step 4** — multiply the two scores together to arrive at an overall 'risk score' for the occurrence. The higher the risk score, the more beneficial it will be to your organisation to retain the particular individual, and the greater the urgency to act. You will need to come to a decision about priorities for action — typically, by establishing a 'threshold' score which will trigger the need to take preventative action.

The benefits of carrying out risk analyses is that they will enable you to build up a picture of the 'hot spots' in your organisation, in terms of its key people, posts and groups of employees. Special retention initiatives targeted at these hot spots should bring particular rewards, and can be justified to the organisation because of the business advantages they will bring.

3.4 The costs of labour turnover

Wastage statistics alone — no matter how specific they are, how well presented, and how well researched in terms of external comparisons — still may not be enough to convince top management that retention initiatives could benefit the organisation. To do this, you may have to attach £ signs to your data.

3.4.1 Costing wastage — when to do it

Rather than dissipate resources in attempting to cost wastage throughout the organisation, you should focus on the target areas. There are two types of wastage worth making an effort for.

- Jobs which account for a large amount of wastage. Examples include staff nurses in a district general hospital, shop floor operatives in a factory, or secretaries in a large headquarters building. The individual posts may not be particularly costly to fill, but the numbers involved — perhaps 100 or more every year — mean that the overall cost of replacement is high.

- Key posts in the organisation — perhaps at a senior management level, or in a specialist area. The cost of finding a replacement for just one of these posts could run into thousands of pounds, or even hundreds of thousands if lost income is taken into account.

3.4.2 Costing wastage — how to do it

IES has published a checklist for costing labour turnover, which can be found in Appendix 2. The checklist includes the following components:

- separation costs
- temporary replacement costs
- recruitment and selection costs
- induction and training costs.

Some of these costs are easier to provide than others, but even the more difficult elements are amenable to estimation. The result will provide a **minimum cost of replacement** for the post in question, and is therefore a particularly useful tool for the HR manager who is trying to persuade his/her organisation to adopt when arguing for retention initiatives aimed at decreasing voluntary wastage rates by a few percentage points.

The IES checklist does not take into account the harder to estimate components of wastage, such as:

- the relative inefficiency of the new employee while he/she is climbing the learning curve
- the disruptive effect on stayers of losing colleagues and adjusting to newcomers
- loss of income
- loss of competitive advantage, particularly if your key employee has gone to a rival company

The reasons why these costs are not included in the checklist are, firstly, the difficulty of quantifying them, and secondly, the danger that they may not be capable of being costed consistently. However, it may be worth making the attempt, as a one-off exercise, for a handful of selected posts in the organisation which are recognised to be of key importance.

4 Why Do People Leave?

In this chapter we will examine:

- the role of voluntary resignations
- some of the commonly used approaches to discovering why employees resign
- common reasons for leaving.

4.1 Voluntary resignations

Voluntary resignations are the least predictable category of staff turnover within organisations and, as a consequence, are often viewed by employers as being unavoidable (particularly if alternative employment has already been secured). For HR planning strategies to be successful, employers have to minimise the number of 'surprise' resignations within their organisations. Many factors, internal and external, influence voluntary resignations, and managers need to determine how much control they have over the underlying causes.

Organisations must have processes in place that give access to reliable data regarding all types of voluntary resignations. The relatively small number of resignations, due to ill health or domestic responsibilities, are largely unavoidable. However, such occurrences should not necessarily be considered as being outside the manager's control: an increase in the number of resignations due to ill heath, for example, could be an indication that the levels of stress at work are also rising, signalling the need for further investigation. There will always be a few individuals who find a new post as a result of being 'head hunted', particularly those with professional expertise whose skills are in short supply. Retaining such individuals presents organisations with a real challenge, and will be discussed in the next section.

Figure 4.1 'Push and pull' in the resignation decision

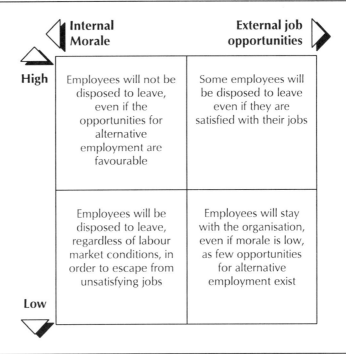

	Internal Morale	**External job opportunities**
High	Employees will not be disposed to leave, even if the opportunities for alternative employment are favourable	Some employees will be disposed to leave even if they are satisfied with their jobs
Low	Employees will be disposed to leave, regardless of labour market conditions, in order to escape from unsatisfying jobs	Employees will stay with the organisation, even if morale is low, as few opportunities for alternative employment exist

Source: IES

The majority of voluntary resignations however, can be attributed to a breakdown in the internal relationship that exists between employer and employee, leading the employee to look to the external job market. Resignation is *then* made easier by a buoyant labour market (see Figure 4.1). Understanding the decision-making process that precedes voluntary resignation is therefore crucial if turnover behaviour is to be understood and subsequently influenced.

4.2 Isolating reasons for leaving

Many larger organisations collect data on reasons for leaving, and usually record these on their computerised HR systems. Often, these data are of limited use only, partly because of problems of missing information and partly because employees tend to offer an unchallenging leaving reason, which the employer wants to hear. '*Post hoc* rationalisation' — justifying the decision to leave, after the event — is also common.

Canvassing the views of leavers regarding their reasons for leaving can help management understand the decision-making process. Two approaches that organisations can employ to compile more informed leavers data are **exit interviews** and **leaver surveys**. Both will yield qualitative, as well as quantitative, information.

4.2.1 Exit interviews

Exit interviews are usually conducted internally, preferably by a 'neutral' representative from Human Resources, who is trained in interviewing. The quality and accuracy of the data collected may be compromised if the interview is conducted by the leaver's existing line manager. Information is sought from leavers during 'face to face' interviews involving a number of 'closed' questions. A disadvantage of the exit interview using closed questions is that leavers have little freedom to express their underlying reasons for leaving. For example, findings reported from exit interviews will often list 'finding another job' as a reason for leaving. However, such a response says nothing about the process that led the employee to take the decision to look towards the external job market. To summarise, when poorly conducted, exit interviews can:

- be time consuming and therefore relatively expensive
- act as a proxy for a counselling service in the final stage of ending the relationship between employee and employer
- be conducted internally
- pressurise leavers to justify leaving
- fail to establish the underlying process that lead to resignation
- Help identify problem areas but rarely effect policy changes.

An example of a 'good practice' exit interview format appears in Appendix 3.

4.2.2 Survey methods

Asking leavers to complete a questionnaire at the time they resign can provide management with more reliable data regarding employees' reasons for leaving. In order to maximise response rates, completed questionnaires should be returned to a 'third party', such as HR, rather than the individual's line manager. A leavers' survey conducted by IES for a large retail company found **the most common reason given for resigning** was:

- the boss's approach to managing staff.

Other important reasons cited for leaving included:

- pay
- the working atmosphere.

In addition to collecting employees' reasons for leaving, the survey sought information regarding leavers' biographical backgrounds, employment histories, levels of job satisfaction and destinations on leaving. The questionnaire also sought suggestions aimed at improving staff retention. **Leavers reported being dissatisfied** with a number of aspects of working for the company but most were related to the way employees were treated. Further analysis of these data enabled IES to establish differences between the views of:

- male and female leavers
- leavers working full and part-time

and

- leavers according to their age groups.

Employee attitude surveys can also be instrumental when conducting a **risk analysis** — as survey data can help organisations spot the early warning signs that often underpin and lead to **unwanted resignation**. During periods of organisational change or mergers it makes good business sense to understand what issues are on employees' minds. Employees' future career intentions can also help identify trends and determine 'pockets' of high turnover risk — attitudinal measures of job satisfaction are widely accepted as being one of the most reliable **indicators of turnover** behaviour. In order to understand the impact that radical changes had on staff within a large manufacturing pharmaceutical company, IES was asked to undertake an employee opinion survey. These data were further explored at a sub-group level, and middle managers and senior professionals were identified as experiencing most pressure at work. Their key concerns were around:

- not having enough time to get their work done
- working longer hours in order to meet their targets
- the adequacy of resources.

They were also found to be:

- more likely to leave within the next two years
- most confident about finding another job if they left the company.

Businesses may also benefit from conducting a survey of 'stayers' in parallel with a 'leavers' survey, and include a number of attitudinal items on the questionnaire **regarding leaving intentions**. The responses from both groups — 'stayers' and 'leavers' — may be examined to determine whether any patterns exist and whether they vary at a sub-group level such as: job type, age group, gender, or length of service. A well-designed survey can help identify high risk groups and the underlying factors (internal and external) that cause dissatisfaction within organisations.

IES was commissioned in response to concern over **high resignation rates** within a large public sector organisation. A survey of leavers and stayers revealed that leavers were generally less satisfied than stayers, and had a different biographical profile. They were more likely to be:

- younger, single, living at home with parents or in rented accommodation and have a shorter length of service

and

- seeking greater job satisfaction, promotion opportunities and challenging work — that used their skills.

Stayers attached more importance to:

- job security
- pay
- flexible working hours.

Leavers were not significantly less satisfied with their **pay** than those who intended to stay, and **pay did not feature** as the most important factor influencing resignation. Key recommendations aimed at reducing unwanted turnover included encouraging strategies intended to improve:

- job content and redesign
- the standards of supervision and management

and

- the way careers are managed.

The above examples illustrate how survey findings can help organisations understand some of the issues which underlie the data and can help demonstrate to employees that the business takes their views seriously. Conducting a survey is not always easy and there are benefits in seeking professional expertise and advice before launching a leavers' survey. Key points that need to be taken into account when considering surveys are:

- the survey must be confidential or, better still, anonymous
- the timing of leavers' surveys, as individuals' memories become distorted even after a short amount of time
- returning the completed questionnaires to a third party
- the added value of surveying a control group (stayers) in parallel with a leavers survey
- the merits of consulting independent professional advice.

4.3 Reasons often given for leaving

In addition to the above examples, IES has carried out work for a range of financial sector organisations and found clerical, administrative and professional staff cited:

'poor promotion prospects'

'not enough job satisfaction'

'poor quality management'

as **the main reasons for resigning.** Less than ten per cent of leavers from each organisation cited 'pay' as a reason for leaving, and fewer than nine per cent from each organisation considered 'increasing pay' would have prevented them from leaving.

The same individuals from the financial organisations were also asked what they feel their employer could have done to **keep them from leaving** and just a few said that increasing their pay would have stopped them from leaving.

There is also substantial research evidence, from within organisations, to show that both those who leave and those who stay with an organisation, express similar levels of dissatisfaction with their **pay**. The examples cited in this chapter illustrate how a number of underlying factors, **other than pay**, were instrumental in the decision making process that preceded voluntary resignation.

Although voluntary resignations may be considered the least predictable category of staff turnover, organisations need not necessarily view them as unavoidable, as many of the reasons cited concerned internal processes and are therefore within an organisation's control. There are a number of **retention strategies** that managers might employ which may influence the process that leads to voluntary resignation and will be discussed in the following section.

5 What Can be Done?

Good organisational health depends, in part, on successfully managing the process of staff renewal. A major challenge facing organisations today concerns managing to achieve a level of turnover that is healthy for both employer and employees. Although employers usually focus their attention towards the costs of high turnover, low turnover also brings its problems. In addition, employers are increasingly aware of the business value of retaining key employees, such as those involved with commercially sensitive work, or experts who have a high market value. Traditional approaches to retention might prove inappropriate or ineffective for such key people. Employers also need to be mindful that certain groups might also have 'special needs' which could vary from sector to sector. Earlier sections have stressed the value of acknowledging that there is a turnover problem, and identifying those causes within an organisation's control. This section is concerned with the extent to which turnover can be influenced by changes to internal policies and practices as a means of retaining a relatively stable, yet flexible, workforce.

5.1 Recruitment and selection

Skill shortages, together with 'hard to fill' vacancies, can often result in organisations recruiting staff who have a high risk of leaving. Evidence shows that new recruits have a higher risk of leaving than employees with a longer length of service. The risk is increased further if applicants are not matched to the vacancy, as this may lead the candidate to form unrealistic expectations of the job. Organisations should, therefore, seek to minimise the risk of 'recruiting turnover' by looking at the effectiveness of their recruitment and selection practices.

Applicants need realistic and honest information, prior to the interview, about both the organisation and the job, to help them form realistic perceptions of the vacancy. Shortlisting methods should be reliable and consistent. A competence-based approach which focuses on the required mix of skills can prove of value here, and can also be useful for providing applicants with feedback.

New recruits' expectations of their jobs need to be managed effectively, otherwise they are likely to become dissatisfied and leave. Organisations need to monitor the views and performance of new recruits.

In summary, key points for organisations to consider are:

- the accuracy of job/person specifications
- the reliability of 'sifting' and 'shortlisting' methods
- the success of current selection and recruitment methods
- turnover rates of new recruits.

5.2 Induction and training

The early experiences of new recruits can be influential in determining the quality and stability of the relationship between employer and employee. Research suggests that job satisfaction established early on can significantly reduce the risk of new recruits becoming disillusioned, which in turn reduces the risk of early resignation. The induction process and early training opportunities are instrumental in helping the new entrant 'settle in' and should be carefully planned and co-ordinated. New recruits (and those who may have been re-deployed into new posts), need to understand exactly what is expected from them, both in job terms and performance. The role of the line manager should not be underestimated during this critical time period. The line manager should ensure support mechanisms are in place that allow newcomers to orient themselves in order for them to begin to make a valuable contribution. Managers should:

- ensure induction happens shortly after joining for all new recruits
- be sure the elements of the job are made clear

- facilitate real learning opportunities, avoiding a 'sheep dip' approach
- be explicit regarding the quality and performance expectations against which newcomers will be measured
- provide the opportunity to meet key people
- ensure the organisational 'map' is understood
- provide regular feedback.

5.3 Job design/content

Employees often report being dissatisfied with aspects of their jobs and say they find their work 'boring'. If we look in more detail at the reasons that underpin their dissatisfaction, we find they are usually unhappy with the lack of:

- control
- responsibility
- variety
- opportunities to use skills
- challenge
- autonomy

that their jobs offer, which may be a consequence of the way jobs have been designed.

Organisations frequently overlook the range of skills employees can offer, particularly those considered to be in 'low' level occupations. Managers need to understand and utilise the full range of employees' skills in order to reduce the amount of 'boredom' in their jobs. Organisations also should be mindful of the difference between 'job enrichment' and 'job enlargement'. The former should provide the individual with more interesting, challenging and varied work, whereas the latter usually involves simply giving the individual more (and too much) to do. Work-related stress, as a result of excessive work pressures, can increase the risks of turnover. Psychologists link three distinct, yet related, sources of stress with job content:

- **role overload** — being asked to perform too many roles to such an extent that none are performed adequately

- **role conflict** — having to perform roles that directly compete with each other, such as health care professionals who have to be providers of care, but also controllers of the costs of that care

- **role ambiguity** — being unclear or confused about what the organisation expects, such as managers being expected to deliver business objectives when priorities keep changing.

Strategies that organisations might employ to maximise the impact of job design and job content on turnover, could include:

- providing opportunities that offer challenge, responsibility and variety for all staff

- encouraging individuals and teams to become aware of their contribution

- having a process that monitors and reviews levels of work-related stress.

One thing is clear from work carried out among specialist or high-skill employees: while they may have high market value, and can command substantial packages, an intrinsically interesting and challenging job is what ultimately motivates them.

5.4 Job satisfaction

Leavers often cite 'lack of job satisfaction' as a reason for resignation. However, a number of elements cluster around what is broadly known as job satisfaction and can often be linked with aspects of job design and content. Commonly accepted components of job satisfaction are:

- the work itself
- line management
- colleagues
- pay
- working conditions/environment.

Employers need to look at the various components to determine whether any action can be taken to improve employees' levels of job satisfaction. Measures of job satisfaction in employee surveys are often good indicators of resignation risk.

5.5 Career progression

Promotion opportunities have become more rare in most organisations, largely as a result of de-layering and flatter structures. Lack of career opportunities are also frequently cited as reasons for resignation. Individuals who feel their contribution goes unrewarded often feel undervalued, which can lead to dissatisfaction and an increase of unwanted turnover. Performance management systems should therefore be seen to be objective and fair, to avoid allegations of 'nepotism'. Employees need to understand the performance criteria against which they are being measured, otherwise they will become dissatisfied. Many employers are now using competence-based appraisal systems to help manage performance. Managing careers presents a real challenge for most employers. Even new recruits, after a short time, often perceive their opportunities with their new employer as being little better than those offered by their previous employer. Careers need to be managed effectively and sensitively and this means conducting appraisals regularly and professionally with agreed actions being followed up. Key areas for attention include making sure that:

- promotions are based upon merit
- performance management systems are fair and fully understood
- employees receive regular feedback on their performance
- appraisals are conducted professionally and regularly, and actions followed up
- the organisation is honest and open about the career progression opportunities that exist.

5.6 Developmental opportunities

Providing employees with opportunities for personal development can help compensate for the lack of promotions within organisations. Quality initiatives, together with the growing number of organisations becoming 'Investors in People', demonstrate that many believe their commercial success, now more than ever, depends upon their workforce. In addition, there are an increasing number of individuals who are linking their training to externally accredited qualifications such as NVQs. Employers need to be realistic regarding the sort of developmental opportunities they can offer, which will vary according to the individual and the business sector. Employees become more 'marketable' both within and outside their organisations as a result of widening their experiences or by developing new skills. Providing good quality training for employees signals that the organisation is prepared to invest in its employees. The likelihood of further training can also act as an inducement to stay with the company.

The appraisal process may facilitate discussion between employees and their line managers that not only reviews past performance, but also looks at the individual's short and longer term aspirations. Generating a personal development plan (PDP), which may or may not be shared with others, is a way of identifying and recording an individual's developmental needs. Mobility may emerge as a problem for 'dual career' couples or for individuals at certain times (such as when children are taking GCSE or 'A' level courses), and PDPs can help in planning for such circumstances. The individual is usually encouraged to 'own' his/her development, with the line manager seeking to deliver and support those aspects of the plan that should benefit both employer and employee. The following points should be borne in mind:

- employees' needs vary — tailor development to fit the individual's needs and aspirations

- use mechanisms such as appraisal to identify development needs

- provide development that is beneficial to both employer and employee

- ensure line managers understand the value of using development as a motivational tool.

5.7 Supervision and management

The line manager's role has changed during recent years. Typically, the line manager now has responsibility for many functions, including 'people management'. The quality of relationships between employees and their line managers is therefore central in managing turnover. Employees' perceptions of their organisation are largely shaped by their day-to-day contact with their line managers. Today's line managers need a whole 'knapsack' of skills, and their behaviour can directly affect employees' levels of morale, job satisfaction, and the risk of turnover. Line managers are a key group of employees who play a pivotal role in retention and they are often targeted for particular attention within organisations. Line managers need to be trained, developed and supported as they represent the 'front line' in the battle against unwanted turnover. They are instrumental in key areas such as:

- selection and recruitment
- induction and training
- job design
- performance management (including pay)
- identifying and facilitating development.

5.8 Pay and benefits

Although pay is an important aspect of an employee's job, research evidence suggests people seldom resign because of their levels of pay, but are more likely to have become dissatisfied with the equity of the pay system. The exception to this rule is very low paid employees, to whom a few pounds a week can make a big difference in quality of life. IES research shows that, in most cases, stayers and leavers within an organisation exhibit no significant differences regarding their levels of satisfaction with their pay — the two groups are usually equally dissatisfied. Once employees have become dissatisfied with aspects of their job and have made the decision to leave, they will then seek to maximise their pay opportunities. Receiving a higher rate of pay from a new employer can therefore be considered an outcome of resignation, rather than pay being the cause — however convenient it may be for the organisation to blame its pay rates for its problems! Pay systems should be seen to be administered fairly and include mechanisms that allow:

- a clear performance criteria to be maintained and monitored
- flexibility to attract and retain employees within a corporate framework
- pay levels linked to the market value
- consistency between managers.

5.9 Retention bonuses

An increasing number of organisations are considering the use of retention bonuses as a tool. These attempt to influence employee behaviour in one of three ways:

1. **To prevent leaving being considered in the first place**: this is unlikely to be effective if no other measures are being taken.

2. **To persuade 'waverers'**: this approach may work with employees who are unhappy, but are looking for an excuse to stay, though less effective with those who have psychologically disengaged.

3. **To defer the decision to leave**: this approach accepts that individuals will leave eventually, and may be effective if the sum on offer is significant enough to convince individuals to stay long enough to complete projects *etc.*

Underpinning the use of such bonuses is a view that they can have the effect of increasing (in the short term) the service the organisation gets from an individual, particularly if they have a valuable set of skills. However, several problems remain unresolved or exacerbated by retention bonuses:

- They can cause resentment among those ineligible for bonuses, either because they (or their post) are not considered 'vital' enough, or because they have not made sufficient 'fuss' compared with others.

- There can be a 'dead-weight' effect, meaning that bonuses might be paid to people in 'high risk' posts who are not disposed to leave, or to individuals who the organisation would not be sorry to lose.

- They can cause an internal 'bidding-up' process whereby different parts of the business seek to make a case that salaries are out of 'synch.' with the market and that retention bonuses are needed to avoid a damaging loss of key people.

- They can be rendered ineffective by predatory employers 'buying out' such bonuses in their enthusiasm to secure the services of particularly valuable individuals.

- They can play havoc with internal relativities and the integrity of grading systems, unless the basis on which they are paid is clear from the start (*ie* are they consolidated/non-consolidated, pensionable/non-pensionable, attached to the post or the person?).

- Unless they have specific eligibility rules (bounded by both job definitions and by time limits on eligibility) they can cease to have impact by being subsumed into the employee's package of perceived benefits.

In some circumstances, retention bonuses can look like a rather blunt instrument: they send out a message that the business is serious about retaining some people, even in the absence of any evidence that they 'work'. What seems clear is that they can only have limited impact by themselves. Unless, in parallel, other approaches to retention are being adopted, it is unlikely that retention bonuses by themselves will yield the expected return.

5.10 Different deals

The shape of future employment and careers is changing. Employers are having to form a realistic view about the length of service they can expect from an employee, particularly specialist staff who can be difficult to attract, retain and manage. For some time we have heard that employers cannot offer 'jobs for life', and that employees have become 'empowered' and are largely encouraged to take control of their own development. Employers are no longer suspicious of 'job hoppers' and there is a growing trend for individuals to have short, varied and discontinuous 'episodes' of work, (often on short-term contracts). Smart organisations are beginning to acknowledge the advantages of introducing different working practices that offer different 'deals' to suit both employee and employer. For some time employers have recognised the value of offering flexible working arrangements for women returners, women wanting part-time work, and mature workers, as these groups offered a solution to skills shortages within certain work areas. Flexible deals include:

- part-time working
- job sharing
- home-working
- casual labour
- subcontracting
- career breaks
- flexitime
- childcare voucher schemes

- seasonal employment
- term-time only working.

During periods of organisational change, such as redundancy, delayering or company mergers, employers are confronted with a number of challenges in order to retain valued and key people, who are likely to feel insecure and vulnerable. Specialists or technical experts with skills such as IT are often at the forefront of employers' minds, and pose a particular challenge. Other valued employees may be those with experience and understanding of an organisation's history, culture and systems, who might be considered to act as organisational or corporate 'glue' and therefore be worthy of special attention. Employers need an understanding of what might motivate different groups and individuals. It is important that *ad hoc* deals do not compromise corporate HR strategies.

Where organisations have identified a risk of losing key employees, which might result in grim commercial consequences, special retention strategies might include:

- share option schemes
- market supplements
- local pay additions, to acknowledge regional differences
- performance-related bonuses
- deferred bonuses, locking in key employees or teams for a time period, or until special projects are completed.

Some of the pay bonus deals may have a 'shelf-life expectancy', and are therefore likely to become eroded by other pay increases.

Experts are key people who value a considerable degree of autonomy in the way they operate, and have been shown to be motivated by intrinsic aspects of their work such as whether:

- their work is seen as worthwhile
- the work is challenging and stretching
- their work uses their skills to the full
- they feel they have control over the content and pace of their work
- they feel they are recognised, valued and trusted.

Organisations should try to deliver 'softer' rewards to such individuals. Promises of career progression, salary increases or financial deals may not motivate those who are known to derive considerable satisfaction from intrinsic aspects of their work, and by knowing their reputations are valued by their peers. Other non-financial benefits might include:

- professional development
- attendance at key conferences
- selective secondment — inter- and intra-organisational
- foreign travel
- assessment/development centres
- careers counselling/workshops
- cross-group project working
- lateral job moves.

5.11 Examples of action taken by employers

While external forces may account for major upward and downward trends in labour turnover, there is evidence to show that organisations can and do reduce wastage with properly targeted retention initiatives. The word 'targeted' is important here, as a general, unfocused retention drive is likely to dissipate resources and be spread too thin to have much tangible benefit. The following examples have been selected to show that retention action **can work**.

- WH Smith targeted sales assistants for a retention initiative, after discovering that replacing a sales assistant (in 1991) cost £2,000. Turnover fell from 40 per cent in 1991 to 24 per cent in 1993 (quoted in IDS Report 661).

- Debenhams introduced a flexible retention initiative called 'Stars' to try to reduce its high wastage rate. The company successfully reduced turnover from over 60 per cent in 1988-89 to well under 40 per cent for 1989-90, and saved £1.6 million as a result (quoted in *Personnel Management*, July 1991).

- A high technology manufacturing company in 'Silicon Valley', California, introduced a turnover study for its manufacturing employees. The study used a mixture of improved information, employment initiatives and reward strategies. At the start of the study, turnover was running at nine per cent; by the end, 27 months later, the rate had decreased to 3.3 per cent (quoted in *Management World*, August 1981).

- In North Manchester Health Care NHS Trust, the pathology manager was concerned that a large proportion of qualified technicians were not returning to work after maternity leave. The trust introduced guidelines on flexible working which enabled managers to offer their staff part-time, job share, or other forms of flexible working. A year on, the pathology department had decreased its leaving rate from 37 per cent to 15 per cent (quoted in *Staff Turnover in NHS Trusts Audit Guide*, 1996).

The message that comes across from these initiatives is that employer action can work, provided that it follows the three **'golden rules'**: firstly, **acknowledge that there is a problem**; secondly, **identify the causes within your control**; and thirdly, **target solutions on these causes**.

The final chapter comprises a brief case study of a company which followed these 'golden rules' in seeking to address a retention problem among some of its IT graduates.

6 Case Study: Retaining IT Graduates

A major IT company was concerned that, while it seemed able to attract recruits to its graduate training programme, its subsequent ability to retain them was poor. This was a particular concern because:

1. Considerable cost and effort went into selecting, recruiting and training each graduate entrant.
2. Given the 'leading edge' nature of some of the work which graduates did, losing gifted people to competitors meant that competitive advantage was being eroded.
3. The disruption to the work of key projects caused by such a loss could put product development back by several months, and was beginning to affect morale.

In an attempt to deal with these issues, the company decided to investigate their retention problems as they affected IT graduates. This involved:

1. examining existing wastage patterns to isolate those graduates at highest 'risk' of leaving
2. conducting interviews with graduates and their managers
3. examining the literature used to attract graduate applicants to vacancies
4. conducting a survey of IT graduates and their attitudes and intentions
5. conducting a parallel survey of leavers.

The company found, perhaps unsurprisingly, that its main losses were among young, single , better qualified graduates. However, contrary to the beliefs of many line managers, dissatisfaction with pay and benefits did not feature strongly as a major reason for leaving. Indeed, comparing the key results from the survey of

Figure 6.1 IT Graduates — attitudes of 'stayers' and 'leavers'

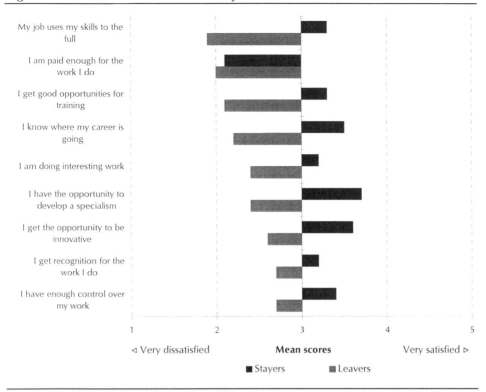

Source: IES

leavers and that conducted among 'stayers', several other factors appeared to be more important in determining resignations.

Figure 6.1 shows the satisfaction scores from the two surveys. The results from the 'stayers' group are, with one exception, positive. Among leavers the scores are far less positive. Indeed, the gaps between some of the scores are highly significant. There was virtually no difference on the issue of pay — with both groups expressing a similar degree of dissatisfaction. The key differences were with issues pertaining to job satisfaction, job content, job design and skill use/development.

These results, coupled with the results of the analysis of recruitment literature, began to send a strong message. The recruitment process, given the imperative to attract the best IT graduates, was 'overselling' some key aspects of the job. Thus, the expectations of some graduates of work autonomy, development opportunities and opportunities to innovate were unrealistically high.

40 The Institute for Employment Studies

As a result of this work, together with a costing exercise, the company reviewed and changed its practices with regard to:

Recruitment and induction: recruitment literature was re-designed to make it more realistic and to avoid over-glamorising jobs. The induction process was changed to involve the introduction of a 'buddy' system by which a graduate from the previous year's intake was assigned to each new recruit to help 'show them the ropes'.

Job design and skill use: graduate development programmes were re-vamped to recognise the importance of project working as a vehicle for learning. Graduates were made more explicitly aware of the role they were expected to play on key projects, were given supervised opportunities to make additional contributions if these were merited, and had the opportunity to reflect on their experience with a mentor after each project experience.

Career management: the company revised its internal job vacancy system to make it more open and informative, it extended the use of personal development planning and assigned mentors to graduate entrants. It also began the selective use of cross-divisional job movement for 'high-flyers', in an attempt to demonstrate that career paths could be lateral as well as vertical.

Line management: much of this work demonstrated that some line managers were much better than others at managing and retaining high quality and marketable graduates. This prompted the company to adjust its line management training content, and to encourage line managers to be 'corporate players' by releasing key staff for company projects or internal promotion.

Within a year of introducing these changes, early losses of IT graduates had been halved, providing the company a more solid foundation on which to base a longer-term contribution from its IT graduate population.

Appendix 1
Costing Labour Turnover Checklist

Institute for Employment Studies

Costing Labour Turnover Checklist

Employee/Grade:...

Minimum entry qualifications and experience:

The Checklist

The checklist represents an inventory of cost headings associated with the turnover and replacement of **one** employee. These headings are grouped into the following categories:

1. Separation Costs
2. Temporary Replacement Costs
3. Recruitment and Selection Costs
4. Induction and Training Costs

Within each category, we have subdivided the cost headings. For **each** cost heading, we would like you to provide a monetary figure representing the current costs that are (or are likely to be) incurred as a result of the turnover and replacement of **one** employee. We have left space in each category for you to add any 'other' cost headings that we have failed to include, but which you feel are important.

In reality, it may be difficult to provide precise figures for some of the costs incurred. In such cases, we would prefer that you include informed estimates rather than leave the form blank. We are interested not only in precise figures, but also in orders of magnitude and broad cost parameters.

Throughout the checklist, it would be extremely helpful if you could make notes to explain any estimates you use in arriving at any of your final figures, particularly:

1. Any assumptions made.
2. Derivation of estimates.
3. Source of data.
4. Difficulty of derivation.

1. Separation Costs

These represent the costs associated with the voluntary resignation process itself. When an individual resigns, the organisation which he or she leaves incurs costs relating to the termination of the contract of employment. This section of the checklist, therefore, is concerned only with these separation costs.

Pay related costs include those cash payments for leave not taken, and for leavers entitled to length of service bonuses. Other costs focus on staff time associated with assisting the leaver to secure alternative employment, *eg* providing references and counselling interviews. The other main element is made up of clerical/ administration time taken up with processing the standard pension and payroll administration, and also any updating and transfer of personnel records.

1. Separation Costs

		£	Notes and Comments
1.1.1	Holiday pay, length of service bonus, *etc.*		
1.1.2	Manager's time: writing references		
1.1.3	Clerical/administration time:		
	pensions administration		
	payroll administration		
	personnel administration		
1.1.4	Interviewer's time: exit interview (counselling)		
1.1.5	Other		
1.2	**Total Separation Costs**		

2. Temporary Replacement Costs

Here we are concerned with the costs generated by the provision of temporary or supplementary cover as a direct consequence of an employee leaving. This will be affected considerably by the period of time for which the vacant post is left unfilled and, therefore, the amount of time that this temporary cover is required.

There are three major elements to the costs of this category. Firstly, there are the direct financial costs associated with the variety of temporary replacement mechanisms available to the employer. Second, there is the costs of the clerical/administration time taken up in arranging temporary cover and the consequent payroll implications. Third, there are the cost implications of experienced staff who are required to provide informal, on-the-job instruction to agency and other temporary staff. This instruction may include details of unfamiliar procedures, equipment *etc*.

2. Temporary Replacement Costs

		£	Notes and Comments
2.1.1	Overtime costs		
2.1.2	Acting-up allowance		
2.1.3	On call/call out allowance		
2.1.4	External agency costs		
2.1.5	Clerical/administration time		
	payroll administration		
	arranging cover		
2.1.6	Formal/informal instruction		
2.1.7	Other		
2.2	**Total Temporary Replacement Costs**		

3. Recruitment and Selection Costs

The costs in this category reflect those incurred in replacing the single, notional leaver. They include both the process of attracting applicants, and that of screening and assessing potential candidates up to the stage when a replacement appointment is made.

Major costs relate to the expenditure associated with the recruitment and selection process. They include the costs of advertising, carrying out medical checks *etc.*, as well as the relevant portion of the salaries of staff employed only as recruiters.

Other costs relate to the clerical and administration time spent processing applications and in the administration of selection interview. In addition, the time spent by other managerial staff who may occasionally be involved in the recruitment and selection process (*eg* on the interview panels) is included as a cost heading.

3. Recruitment and Selection Costs

		£	Notes and Comments
3.1.1	Advertising costs		
3.1.2	Applicants' expenses		
3.1.3	Recruiter's pay and costs		
3.1.4	Checking references		
3.1.5	Administration of selection tests		
3.1.6	Medical examinations		
3.1.7	Clerical/administration time:		
	processing applications		
	interview administration		
3.1.8	Management time		
3.1.9	Other		
3.2	**Total Recruitment and Selection Costs**		

4. Induction and Training Costs

These costs represent those incurred, after appointment, in establishing the new incumbent in his or her post, and developing their skills and expertise to the point at which they cease to be a net cost to the employing organisation.

These include the costs of equipping, in practical terms, the new employee to do their job, as well as any relocation or temporary accommodation costs that may be necessary during the initial weeks of their employment. The cost of off-the-job training, including short courses, day release *etc.* where appropriate, and the relevant portion of the salary of training staff are also included. A further inclusion is that proportion of the recruit's salary which is paid to them prior to their reaching a normal level of operational efficiency in their new job. This, of course, will vary according to the previous experience of the recruit.

Clerical/administration time involved in the processing of many of the activities is also included, as is the time of 'inductors' and on the job training/coaching inputs made informally by supervisors and/or colleagues during the initial period of employment. The costs of equipment and materials may be represented by the costs of using service-designated equipment for training purposes, and the associated waste of non-reusable material.

4. Induction and Training Costs

		£	Notes and Comments
4.1.1	Relocation costs		
4.1.2	Temporary accommodation		
4.1.3	Uniform/equipment		
4.1.4	Formal, off-job training		
4.1.5	Trainer's pay		
4.1.6	Training equipment/material		
4.1.7	Non-productive recruit's pay		
4.1.8	Clerical/administration time		
4.1.9	Temporary accommodation administration		
4.1.10	Pension administration		
4.1.11	Payroll administration		
4.1.12	Personnel administration		
4.1.13	On-job training: inductor's time (including colleagues)		
4.1.14	Other		
4.2	**Total Induction and Training Costs**		

5. Total Costs

	£	Notes and Comments
Separation Costs		
Temporary replacement cost		
Recruitment and selection costs		
Induction and training costs		
Total turnover costs		

The Institute for Employment Studies

Appendix 2. Retention Risk Analysis

RETENTION RISK ANALYSIS

Confidential to the Institute for Employment Studies

Line Manager Assessment Form

In order to quantify the risk of key employees leaving the business, and to estimate the consequences or impact of their doing so, we are conducting a pilot risk analysis exercise. The aim is to help the company to prioritise pre-emptive actions which might be necessary to prevent the losses of key employees.

As part of this pilot exercise, we would be grateful if you could take the time to complete the attached form for **each** of the employees who report direct to you.

This exercise is being conducted on a **confidential** basis, and none of the information you give will be used beyond the confines of this pilot exercise.

The Institute for Employment Studies

Confidential

Retention risk analysis: Likelihood

Employee name: ....

On the basis of what you know about this employee, please rate them on the following factors:

1. Age:	Under 28 ☐	29 – 35 ☐	Over 35 ☐	
2. Status:	Married ☐	Single ☐	Separated ☐	
3. Children:	Yes ☐	No ☐		
4. Morale:	Very good ☐	Moderate ☐	Poor ☐	
5. Attrition risk:	Would leave now if s/he could ☐	May leave in next 2 yrs ☐	Unlikely to leave in next 2 yrs ☐	

Retention risk analysis: Likelihood

Employee name: ....

Think about the consequences or impact of this employee leaving the company tomorrow. Please rate this eventuality on the following scales:

	High		Moderate		Low	
1. Impact on product/ service delivery:		☐		☐		☐
2. Ease of replacement: (internal or external)		☐		☐		☐
3. Costs of replacement:		☐		☐		☐
4. Advantage to competitors: (skills, knowledge, expertise)		☐		☐		☐

The Institute for Employment Studies

Appendix 3.   Exit Interview Questionnaire

Exit Interview Questionnaire
Good Practice Example

A. General information

Name: ....

Job title: ....

Grade: ....

Department/location: ....

Age group:

24 and under	25 to 34	35 to 44	45 to 54	55 to 64	65 and over
❏	❏	❏	❏	❏	❏

Length of service: ....

Gender: Male   Female

                             ❏   ❏

Ethnic group: ....

B. Working in the organisation

1. What first attracted you to work for the organisation?

....

....

....

2. Were your expectations met?

....

....

....

3. What was the best aspect of working in the organisation?

....

....

....

4. What was the worst aspect?

....

....

....

5. If you could change something within the organisation what would it be?

....

....

....

C. Where are you going? (Leaving destination)

Please indicate the type of organisation you are joining

❑ An organisation in the same sector

❑ An organisation in a different sector

❑ Further study

❑ Self employment

❑ Not working

❑ Other *(please specify)* ....

D. Location of work

❑ Local areas

❑ Within 10 mile radius

❑ Elsewhere (please specify) ....

E. Reasons for leaving

Please indicate your main reason(s) for leaving:

❑ Dissatisfaction with pay

❑ Dissatisfaction with conditions of service

❑ Lack of promotion/career development

- ❏ Lack of training and development

- ❏ Partner moving out of area

- ❏ Other domestic reasons

- ❏ Difficulty travelling to and from work

- ❏ Flexibility of working hours

- ❏ Workload/stress

- ❏ Dissatisfaction with management style

- ❏ Work environment

- ❏ Nature of work/job satisfaction

- ❏ Way work is organised

- ❏ End of contract

- ❏ Insufficient challenge

- ❏ Maternity

- ❏ Unsolicited offer

- ❏ Other (please specify)

2. What was the most important reason for your leaving?

....

....

....

3. What, if anything, would have encouraged you to stay?

....

....

....

F. Any other comments

....

....

....

....

....

....

....

....

....

....

Thank you for taking the time and trouble to complete this questionnaire. The information that you have provided will be used in turnover statistics and feedback to senior management to help in reviewing personnel and management procedures.

Bibliography/References

Atkinson J, Rick, J, Morris S, Williams M (1996), *Temporary Work and the Labour Market*, IES Report 311

Computer Economics (1995), *Computer Staff Salary Survey*, published by Computer Economics

CSO (1996), *Social Trends 26*, Cental Statistical Office, London

Employment Policy Institute (1996), *Employment Audit*, Issue 2, pp.18-19, Tables 2-2b

Harrop A, Moss P (1994), 'Working Parents: Trends in the 1980s', *Employment Gazette*, 102(10), pp.343-352

Help the Aged (1995), *The Help the Aged Senior Care Survey*, cited in *IRS Employment Trends* 576, January

IER (1995), *Review of the Economy and Employment: Occupational Assessment*, Institute for Employment Research, University of Warwick

IPD (1996), *Labour Turnover, 1996 Survey Results*, Institute of Personnel and Development

IRS (1996), 'Benchmarking and Managing Labour Turnover', *Employee Development Bulletin*, 75, Industrial Relations Service

IRS (1997), 'Benchmarking Labour Turnover: an update', *Employee Development Bulletin*, 87, Industrial Relations Service

King P (1996), 'Workforce Planning: Keeping the baby boomers on board', *Health Service Journal*, 6 June

MCG (1996), *Audit of Personnel Activities and Costs*, National HR Database, published by MCG

ONS (1997), *Labour Market Trends*, Vol. 105, No. 9, September, Office for National Statistics

PAS (1995), *Skill Needs in Britain*, published by Public Attitude Surveys on behalf of Department for Education and Employment

Remuneration Economics (1995), *National Management Salary Survey*, published with the Institute of Management

Sly F (1993), 'Women in the Labour Market', *Employment Gazette*, 10/93, pp.483-502

Useful addresses

Institute of Management, Management House, Cottingham Road, Corby NN17 1TT. 01536 204222

Institute of Personnel and Development, IPD House, Camp Road, Wimbledon SW19 4UX. 0181 971 9000

MCG, 11 John Street, London WC1N 2EB. 0171 242 3665

PAS Ltd, Rye Park House, London Road, High Wycombe HP11 1EF. 01494 532771